Funny Rhymes for Humorous People or Humorous Rhymes for Funny People

Funny Rhymes for Humorous People or Humorous Rhymes for Funny People

Malcolm E. Timms

To order additional copies of this book, contact:
Xlibris Corporation
0-800-644-6988
www.xlibrispublishing.co.uk
Orders@xlibrispublishing.co.uk
302467

CONTENTS

Holes In The Road

The road outside my house I know
Is where the workmen like to go.
The Gasboard sent some men to dig
Three holes: two small, one very big.

They dug them deep,
They dug them true,
Then thought what else they should do.
Three weeks later they came back
And filled them in with hot tarmac.

Seven days later, what a surprise!
More men digging before my eyes.
Were these the same men back again?
No, sewage men to check each drain.

A row of holes dug trim and neat
At intervals of fifty feet.
When they finished three days late
They left the surface in a state.

Driving there now was no fun.
Suspension's ruined, damage done.
Sue the council!
Is that wise?
Council tax is bound to rise.

Monday morning, nine o'clock,
Council men cause traffic block.
When at last the job is done
A smooth road glimmers in the sun.

Two days later more men seen.
They're digging holes behind a screen.
When they emerge the road is flat
Thanks to Murphy, Mick and Pat.

'Whose turn next?' I hear you say.
The water men can't stay away.
They bring new pipes, turn off the main,
Then put everything back again.

Electricity is such a boon
Look out! Their men are coming soon.
Their holes are of a special type
To carry cable in a pipe.

But now they've finished, all work done.
The workmen all have had their fun.
The road is open, give three cheers!
The surface now will last for years.

But as I gaze from my front gate
I know I mustn't celebrate.
The Gasboard men are back once more
I go inside and close my door.

Garden Weeds

What wondrous things are garden weeds!
They don't need you to plant bulbs, corms or seeds.
When other plants wither and fade in the heat
Garden weeds will flourish a-treat.

They'll grow in the ground, they'll grow in a wall,
In a hanging basket one grew two feet tall
Among geraniums it managed to sprout
And I fell off a ladder while digging it out.

Some weeds have spikes as sharp as a pin.
Others are spiteful and sting your skin.
They'll penetrate clothing and cause you to scratch
And leave an unsightly blotchy patch.

Now some weeds are lucky, I suppose.
They grow right under a thorny rose
And when I try to pull them free
I scratch my arm or claw my knee.

Some folk I know will try to advance
Their garden display when they talk to their plants,
But the opposite strategy does not apply:
Ignore your weeds, they won't curl up and die.

Some lawns are like a snooker baize,
Yet leave them uncut for just two days
And daisies spring up overnight
Festooning the green with yellow and white.

Weeds can look attractive with colourful flowers
And they'll grow from nothing in less than twelve hours.
But why must they occupy my flowerbed?
I think they should choose somewhere else instead.

It's out in the countryside where they belong
Where they can grow both big and strong.
They can stay there forever, they don't need a lease
And leave me to garden in calmness and peace.

The Hair Of Alfie Binns

Alfie Binns was born so small
His head was bald, no hair at all.
As he grew up the hair appeared:
By twenty-one he'd grown a beard.
His hair grew matted, thick and long
His mother said: 'It looks all wrong.
You really are a dreadful sight.
Enough to give your Gran a fright.
'Go to the Barber's. Have it cut!'
But Alfie liked his hairy nut.
At thirty-one he settled down
And married Jane from down the town.
Now Jane she liked her man's hair neat
And in the kitchen made him seat
Himself upon a wooden stool.
'Short hair now!' That was her rule.
With comb and clippers once each week
She cut it short down to his cheek
By forty-one his hair was thin:
Most indeed grew on his chin.
Where once had been a frizzy mop
A round bald patch appeared on top
Now that patch has grown so big
Alfie has to wear a wig.

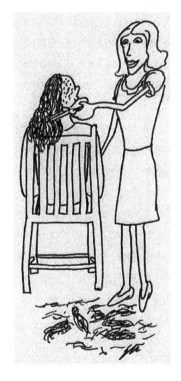

Perseverance

When Jack took up the violin
His arms were short, his fingers thin.
He first tried plucking E and A:
The teacher turned her head away.
'Pluck less hard you silly boy!
That's an instrument not a toy!'
Jack said 'Sorry' for his error
Then ran home in deadly terror.
His mother said: 'Now dry those tears.
You're doing well for seven years.
I'll find you somewhere else to play.'
And so it was next Saturday
He started learning with Miss Tadd
Who found she really liked the lad.
Now the lessons went much better
And Jack learned another letter.
He plucked well on A and E
And soon he learned the third string, D.
Next he learned string number four:
'Jolly good! There are no more!'
He practised hard from day to day,
Pizzicato all the way.
New notes now he had to learn
By pressing fingers down in turn.
Now all day he pleased his Ma
With Twinkle, Twinkle Little Star.
Bowing was his next advance:

Check the grip, hold the stance.
New sounds came sustained and bright;
He kept the neighbours up all night.
To get it right was very hard
And so he practised in the yard.
The cats came in from miles around
Just to hear this wondrous sound.
But perseverance brings rewards:
Soon he had to tread the boards.
His teacher asked him: 'Will you play
For our School fete on 9th of May?'
So Jack agreed and took his chance
Accompanying a country dance.
And when he'd done up went a cheer.
People shouted: 'Over here!'
He signed their programmes, took the praise;
This really was the best of days.
Now at that fete was Mr Hoole,
The man who ran the music school.
So Jack signed up, a budding star
And soon he led the orchestra.
And so to college he progressed,
Exams, degrees, like all the rest,
But Jack was special and his name
Became well-known and spread his fame.
He played in halls throughout the land:
Quartet, orchestra, large string band.

Now he's in the U.S.A.
Giving concerts every day.
His arms once short, are now quite long,
His fingers deft and very strong.
He's made the grade, he's walking tall:
A fine example to us all.

The General Election

Vote for the future society.
Consider the Parties, but vote for me.

Travel by river, road, rail or plane
Who's going to improve them? I have the brain.

Taken to hospital, wait for nine hours.
Who can cut time waste? I have the powers.

Standards are declining they say
I have the answer: ten-hour school day.

On theft and burglary I have the line:
All burglars in bed by half-past nine.

Muggings are common. The system's too lax
Tie naughty boys' hands behind their backs.

Waste disposal is quite a concern:
Recycle everything. Don't ever burn.

On foreign relations my policy's clear:
My Aunt in Gibraltar can sleep without fear.

Grow our own food and cut imports down.
Give E.U. Commissioners reason to frown.

Trade with America, China, Peru.
Decide for ourselves what we want to do.

In pounds and pence our bills should be paid.
Temperature's Fahrenheit not Centigrade.

Political speeches should last half the time
So cut out the waffle and write them in rhyme.

So cast your vote on election day,
But be sure it's for me: don't throw it away.

Buying A Second-Hand House

When buying a house it's a good idea
To hear what is said with a critical ear.
They'll tell you the good bits, skip over the bad:
'Leaving this house will make us so sad!'

The garden is small, 'It's a manageable size.
The damp parts grow marrows, I once won a prize.'
The fence posts are rotten, 'I took the fence down.
It affords a fine view of the neighbouring town.'

I want to grow heather, 'We have lots of rain.
Buried chunks of old concrete help the soil drain.
That crack in the wall is plaster shrinking.'
I think that side of the house is sinking.

'The draft from the chimney keeps the air clear.'
A gale blew the chimney pot down last year.
'The bedrooms are spacious as well you can see.'
There are no fitted wardrobes, that's more work for me.

'The central heating is powered by the sun,
The solar panels are really quite fun.'
But now it is cloudy, the house is stone cold.
It's hardly surprising it hasn't been sold.

'The kitchen appliances are such a boon,
But we're taking them with us. We're moving quite soon.
Our neighbours were friendly they now live abroad.
He threatened my wife with a samurai sword.

This house has character, poise and style!'
The work that needs doing would cost us a pile.
They have coffee brewing, they're baking new bread.
I must pay attention to all that is said.

THE MAIDEN AND THE SOLDIER

A maiden met a soldier.
That soldier he was bold.
The maiden she was twenty,
The soldier he was old.

The maiden she was thrifty
And saw his medals bright:
The soldier he was manly
And saw a pretty sight.

Now maidens who are thrifty
Always think ahead:
Flutter his amusements,
But never go to bed.

One night when they were walking
The weather turned quite bad.
The sky turned black as thunder,
The maiden looked quite sad.

And so into an inn they went
And shared a glass of ale.
The soldier looked quite rosy,
But the maiden she grew pale.

'What shall we do on such a night?'
She asked with manner mild.
'We cannot venture out from here,
The weather is too wild.'

'We'll rent a room and stay the night.'
He answered with intent.
'And by tomorrow morning
This storm it will relent.'

When upstairs her coat came off,
Likewise her blouse of silk
Her eyes were blue, her lips were red,
Her arms were white as milk.

Looking down he spied with fright
Emblazoned on her vest
In jet black letters M.O.D.
Right across her chest.

'What mean these letters that I see
So bold and oh so black ?'
'For three months you've been A.W.O.L.
I've come to take you back.'

Now he languishes in jail:
This tale he would unweave.
The moral of the story
'Don't go absent without leave'.

PAINTING THE FORTH BRIDGE

There's a man in Scotland who's working very hard.
He works from his feet, but gets paid by the yard.
He works from January through to December,
But just when he started he can't remember:
For he's painting the Forth Bridge from end to end.
He paints all the straight bits and every bend.
He paints every girder, every rivet, bolt and pin
And just when he's finishing it's time to begin.

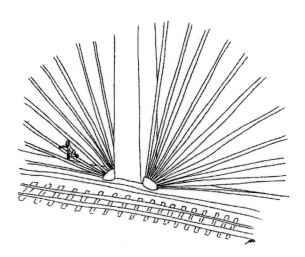

DOUBLE YELLOW LINES

I wear sandals smart and neat.
Shoes are the prisons of the feet.
Traffic; passing: lorry, van;
I'm waiting at a pelican.
I'll cross the road when it is clear.
A double yellow line says 'Don't park here!'
The traffic stops, my light turns green.
I look around, survey the scene.
Crowds move forward in great haste:
'Hurry please, no time to waste!'
I step forward with the rest,
But though I try my very best
I can't obey the flashing sign:
I'm stuck fast to the yellow line.
I lift my foot to extricate
My sandal, but it's now too late.
The light has changed, the traffic flows.
What can I do? Why, Goodness knows!
My brow is furrowed, lips are pursed.
The second line now joins the first
One on toe, the other on heel:
'This situation is unreal.'
Right foot flaming, feeling faint,
Attached to the road by strips of paint.
Left foot kicking, now joins the fray:
Free its fellow, walk away.
Kicking hard, but out of luck;

Both feet now are firmly stuck.
As I move my paint lines lengthen,
Make my resolution strengthen.
I must win. I'll use my brain.
I'll kick these paint strips down the drain.
Now I'm dancing on the grate.
'Are you in trouble? I'll help you mate.'
He pins the paint with his umbrella.
He really is a splendid fella.
First the left foot, then the right.
I'm free at last! Oh, what delight
For all line painters a simple code:
Make sure your paint stays on the road.

Junk Mail

Early each morning around about eight.
(Sometimes he's early, sometimes he's late)
We see our postman come down the road
Staggering under a heavy load.
He leans right over to open our gate
Burdened right down by such a great weight.
But what is he pushing through my front door?
Is it worth picking up from the floor?
I count seven items addressed to me.
Are any worth reading? We'll just have to see.
The Reader's Digest is happy to say
My name has gone forward. It's my lucky day.
But where it's been forwarded I am not sure.
I'll wait till another card comes through my door.
I'm a 'valued customer' with one bank account.
And now they will lend me a large amount.
Dial Direct guarantees a cheap quote,
But I don't own a car, a van or a boat.
There's a time-share in Scotland that might just appeal,
But I must go to Swindon to sign for the deal.
There's a brochure offering low-price C.D.s.
They'll send them out promptly with no postage fees.
A finance company will buy part of my home.
As part of the package there's a holiday in Rome.
There's a leaflet promoting an adjustable bed.
I can raise or lower my feet or my head,
But I'm only thirty and can sleep anywhere:

In a bed, a bunk, a tent or a chair.
Now all these items arrived with my name,
But most of my friends will receive just the same.
Now junk mail is wasteful, I'm sure you'll agree.
Each road costs a branch, each town costs a tree.
Forests are depleted day by day:
The junk mail discarded or just thrown away.

WHEN SANTA GOT STUCK UP THE CHIMNEY

When Santa got stuck up the chimney
He began to shout:
'I've got cheese rolls and beer so leave me in here
And don't try and pull me out.
I've gifts for you all, both big and small
So reach down the chimney and take 'em
I like roast beef and mustard, Christmas pudding and custard
So someone get cracking and bake 'em!'

Hypochondria

I know a man who's incredibly sad.
You see, his health has always been bad.
He suffered through childhood measles and mumps,
Pimples and rashes, depressions and bumps.

I think he's always seeking attention.
He's had every ailment you care to mention.
He had tennis elbow and housemaid's knee;
From coughs and colds he's seldom free.

He collapsed in a heap on Tesco's floor
When he stubbed his toe on a heavy glass door.
He claimed he'd not seen it; the shop was to blame,
But I can see through him: he's always the same.

While staying at Southend he went on the pier,
The woodwork was slippery, it made him feel queer.
The wind and the sea spray affected his brain
And he had to return to the shore on the train.

In London he wanted to go on 'The Eye'.
The weather was perfect, sunny and dry.
But when his capsule was suspended aloft
His head went all dizzy, his knees went all soft.

His diet is strange, I think you'll agree.
He won't drink cocoa, coffee or tea.
He buys bottled water and drinks it cold,
But how long has it been bottled? It could be quite old.

He will not eat chicken and eggs he won't touch,
For chickens have foul-pest; the risk is too much.
He won't eat fresh apples unless they've been peeled
In case they've been sprayed in the orchard or field.

Now if you resemble this man that I know,
Consider your future; which way you should go.
Life's too short to worry, put your diet away.
Eat, drink and be merry, enjoy every day.

The Dustman

When I was a boy the dustman came
Each Monday morning, always the same.
Really early, outside it was dark;
The dogs in the district all started to bark.
He'd pick up my bin of galvanized steel,
Onto his shoulder, carry not wheel.

Then at the dustcart he'd 'empty my trash:
Papers and bottles, bits of old ash.
All in together no sorting it out.
The Council will take it of that there's no doubt.
I remember old Joe, a jovial bloke,
When taking my dustbin he told me this joke:
'Do you know' he asked' what has eight wheels and flies? ..
Two corporation dustcartsl' What a surprise.
Galvanized bins were expensive to make
So plastic replaced them for cheapness' sake.
My dustman then was good old Jack.
He emptied my bin but still brought it back.
Now we have no bin at all.
A plastic sack hangs on the wall.
Paper and metal we must separate;
Food bits make compost, it's most fortunate.
The recycle people we must all thank
For bottles and jars now have their own bank.
Each Monday morning outside our front door
Our bags are collected, we see them no more.
But what's in these bags now? I really can't say.
It's lucky the dustman still takes them away.

SNORING

(Dedicated to Fred and Rita Payne)

Come home weary, full of care.
Slippers on, easy chair.
Wife comes in with cup of tea.
Relaxation! Ecstasy!

Telly spouting evening news.
Settle down to have a snooze.
Feet stretch out across the floor:
Wake up dear! You've started to snore!'

After dinner washing-up.
Telly highlights . . . F.A. cup.
Take no interest, dulls my brain.
'Wake up dear! You're snoring again!'

Half past ten and time for bed.
Go upstairs and rest my head.
Kick off slippers on the floor:
'Remember dear, you mustn't snore!'

Beads of sweat on forehead glisten.
Maybe I'll stay awake and listen.
Dozing sweetly! Dreamy joys:
'Can't you stop that dreadful noise?

There you lie in slumber deep.
How am I supposed to sleep?'
Lie there silent for her sake.
She's now snoring I'm awake.

Half past six, alarm clock bleep
Must get up, no time to sleep.
Solution: if you wish to doze
Place a peg upon your nose.

SHOPPING

Women will shop whenever they can.
But it's totally different for a man.
I once met a man who said with gloom:
'My wife could shop in an empty room.'

Women go shopping a bargain to find.
Men would much rather be left behind.
Women check prices one place with another.
Men just pay up; they don't really bother.

Women like trying on dresses and shoes.
Men buy ·magazines, papers and booze.
Women will haggle to bring down the price
Men just pay up, they never ask twice.

Women like fashions, the latest new styles.
They buy lots of magazines; keep them in piles.
Men mostly opt for a simpler life.
They leave the clothes shopping up to their wife.

Now if you're a woman or if you're a man
Read these lines and decide if you can
If what I have said is false or true.
When there's shopping to be done what do you do?

The Nation's New Toy

Walking down a country lane,
Going to London on the train,
Even standing in the rain;
You see them.

In a park sat on a bench,
Workmen standing in a trench,
Even people speaking French;
Observe them.

On a pavement in the town
Shoppers walking up and down,
Businessmen with heavy frown;
Regard them.

Children riding on a bus,
Anxious mums begin to fuss,
Grumpy tradesmen swear and cuss;
You hear them.

Young girl chatters to her boy,
Tells him he's her hope and joy,
Though in public she's not coy;
Amazing.

People standing in a look,
Horserace punters in a stew,
Even in a public 100;
Surprising.

With all these folk there is a link.
Now just you stop and have a think.
I'll give a clue, there's no coin clink;
Just buttons.

But there's one thing these folk hold dear,
In fact they hold it to their ear,
Parade in public without fear;
Their mobile.

The mobile phone is such a boon.
They say we'll each own one quite soon.
Each one with its special tune;
Annoying.

In this matter I stand alone.
I do not own a mobile phone
Their constant bleepings make me groan;
Expunge them!

GROWING OLD UNSTEADILY

I celebrate my birthday.
It comes round each four years.
Strange this is I reckon,
The other three it disappears.

The 29th of February
Is my actual birth date.
The 28th was predicted,
I turned up rather late.

I have a son named Rupert
And he is thirty-three.
As I am only sixteen
He's much older than me.

His daughter who is four years
Was christened Amy Paige.
Now when she reaches twenty
We'll both be the same age.

My wife says she is sixty
Might well be my own Gran
For while I'm only sixteen
I'm still a smart young man.

My firm has just retired me,
They have an age point rule,
But I am only sixteen
And should be still at school.

After two more birthdays
Eighteen will be score.
I then may join the Army,
Go through the pub front door.

But I did national service
And as for drinking beer
You could fill a petrol tanker
With the pints I drink each year.

When others born the same year as me
Announce they're eighty-four
I shall be just twenty-one
I'll get the key of the door.

Physiques

Some folk are big, some folk are small.
Some folk are short, some folk are tall.
Some folk are thin, others are fat.
Why can't they accept it and leave it at that?
The curly-haired lady; for straight hair she longs
While the lady with straight hair will use curling tongs.
Many brunettes would prefer to be fair
While blondes and red-heads darken their hair.
Some men grow moustaches; others a beard,
But their heads have bald patches which seems really weird.
Health clubs and diet sheets help people slim.
'Do exercises, cycle and swim.'
But millions are starving and suffer ill-health
While overweight people squander their wealth.
Now if you consider your physique is wrong:
Your hair the wrong colour, too short or too long;
Your vital statistics are in the wrong place;
Why not just accept it, put a smile on your face.

THE BALLAD OF SUSIE GREEN

Young Susie Green. while cutting cheese,
Dropped a knife between her knees.
The knife-blade did not hurt her skin,
But slit her jeans where they were thin.

'Now: thought Susie, ' What to do?
There must be someone I can sue.
My jeans are torn, that's just not fair.
I must demand a brand new pair.'

Now as she mused on this idea
She thought her leg was feeling queer.
'This knife has set my nerves a-jangle.
Now I'll see what I can wangle.'

She phoned her doctor, told the tale
And finished with a dreadful wail.
The doctor prescribed pills and rest.
'A week off work' that would be best.

Now at home she watched T.V.
Claims Assisted would without fee
Gain their clients compensation.
They were the best firm in the nation.

With shaking hand she wrote her tale
Then sent it off by first-class mail.
For six long weeks there came no word.
'This situation is absurd!'

Then at last they sent a man.
'I will do everything I can.'
But all this time she'd had not pay.
'Things should not turn out this way!'

Six weeks without eating dinner;
Susie now was growing thinner.
When at last the case was tried
Susie's lawyer sat and sighed.

The wise old judge threw out the case.
For Susie now was in disgrace.
She'd lost her job, she'd cost to find.
This situation was a bind.

But folk like Susie shouldn't win.
Her cheating left her poor and thin.
Susie schemed a cunning plot,
But she was green, the judge was not.

Unwelcome Friends

I must be the world's most popular bloke.
I'm deadly serious, it isn't a joke.
By millions I'm favoured ahead of the rest.
They reckon I'm wonderful, simply the best.
The quest of my fans peaks on hot summer days
When it's humid and sticky; in the garden I laze.
It's too hot for work so I lie in the sun.
'Come boys,' they say. 'It's time for some fun.'
This unusual appeal is hard to condone.
Indeed, I wish they'd leave me alone;
For the millions that mob me wherever I am
Are not named Georgina, Rachel or Pam.
They're not Angelinas, Janets or Pats,
But midges, mosquitoes and blood-thirsty gnats.
I try to repel them with lotions and creams,
But these make no difference, or so it seems.
They bite through the coating and into my skin.
Whatever I try I just can't win.
Now during the war when mines were afloat
With magnetic attraction to blow up a boat;
A device was invented that pushed them away.
The shipping survived for another day.
But such equipment, though alright at sea,
Would not be helpful on land for me.
Gnats and mosquitoes have no magnetism.
I must think of another way I can deal with 'em.
A slow burning candle with perfumed scent

Was once used by campers to clear their tent.
Some lights will attract them and cause them to dive,
But if I'm in the district they just eat me alive.
So if anyone knows of a viable plan
To bring relief to this much-bitten man,
Just tell me how to avoid this strife
And I'll be your friend for the rest of your life.

If I Was A Sportsman

If I was a sportsman I'd show off my skills:
Play ballgames, do athletics without any pills.
I'd demonstrate fitness, show muscular powers
And train every evening for more than two hours.

I'd tackle karate, wrestle and box
Wear a black belt, white vest and green socks.
My opponent would tremble and fall to the floor.
I'd stand there victorious to hear the crowd's roar.

In tennis I'd play with incredible pace
And win every point by serving an ace.
In doubles my partner would follow my lead
And try to match my fantastic speed.

In football I'd be striker and lead the front line
Scoring the goals with ball skills so fine.
Or maybe as goalie I'd save every shot
And win the games that way as likely as not.

In cricket I'd bowl with prodigious pace
Or whack the ball firmly all over the place.
And when my side's fielding, I'd take every catch,
Run out my opponents, be man of the match.

In snooker I'd pot balls in every pocket.
My shots would make them go like a rocket.
With skill and accuracy I'd handle my cue
And show other players what they ought to do.

I'd swim for my nation in backstroke and fly,
Breaststroke and freestyle, through the water I'd fly.
Somersault gracefully as I'd dive from the boards;
The judges amazed, each spectator applauds.

I'd be a great sprinter, at long distance I'd run
And beat every rival from under the sun.
I'd throw the discus, the hammer as well
In any event I'd be bound to excel.

But, I'm not a sportsman, it has to be said.
So I'll stay in my lounge and watch telly instead.

Lightning Source UK Ltd.
Milton Keynes UK
UKOW051832300911

179553UK00004B/66/P